DAILY LIFE

A Cowboy in the Wild West

Other Books in the Daily Life Series:

DAILY LIFE

A Cowboy in the Wild West

Adam Woog

KIDHAVEN PRESS

THOMSON

✦

GALE

Detroit • New York • San Diego • San Francisco
Boston • New Haven, Conn. • Waterville, Maine
London • Munich

For my Dad, a cowboy at heart all his life.

Library of Congress Cataloging-in-Publication Data

Woog, Adam, 1953–
  A Cowboy in the Wild West / by Adam Woog.
    p. cm. — (Daily life)
Includes bibliographical references.
Summary: Discusses the cowboy in the Old West, his dress,
manner and daily activities.
    ISBN 0-7377-0990-1 (hardback : alk. paper)
1. Cowboys—West (U.S.)—History—Juvenile literature.
2. Cowboys— West (U.S.)—Social life and customs—Juvenile
literature. 3. Ranch life—West (U.S.)—Juvenile literature. 4.
West (U.S.)—Sociaz life and customs—Juvenile literature. [1.
Cowboys. 2. Ranch life—West (U.S.) 3. West (U.S.)—Social life
and customs.] I. Title. II. Series.
  F596 .W73 2002
  978—dc21

2001007203

Contents

Cowboys in the Old West

The romantic picture of a cowboy in the Old West is a familiar one. Cowboys rode the range, slept under the stars, fired six-shooters, and wore spurs that jingle-jangle-jingled. Thanks to this image, cowboys came to symbolize independence, pride, and personal freedom.

This image was never completely true, however. A cowboy's life was mostly the difficult, dirty work of herding cattle on horseback. His bosses demanded much but paid him little. His entire world was the ranch he worked on and the trail he rode. Except on special occasions, other cowboys were his only human company. Furthermore, although humor and danger existed in a cowboy's life, most of the time it was dull routine.

On the other hand, there was always some truth in the romantic image. Many cowboys of the Old West would never have considered surrendering the ability to ride their horses for miles across wide prairies, to sleep beneath the stars, or to watch the sun set behind distant mountains. To them, it was the only life.

A weary cowboy watches over his cattle.

The Rise of the Cowboy

Both cattle and horses were brought to North America by Spanish explorers and settlers centuries before Old West cowboys existed. Spanish cowboys were called **vaqueros**. The cowboys of the American West borrowed many customs and styles from them.

The traditions of the vaquero influenced the American cowboy.

The American cowboy did not exist in large numbers until after 1865, when soldiers returning from the Civil War found work on the ranches of the West, mostly Texas. These ranches created huge herds of cattle by collecting wild animals that roamed freely on the prairies.

Ranch owners knew that big cities such as New York and Chicago were good markets for the meat these cattle could provide. It was not practical to bring the cattle "on the hoof" all the way to these cities, however.

The solution was to herd them across the plains to "cow towns," settlements that had brokers who bought cattle and sent them by train elsewhere. These mass migrations of cattle were called trail drives. The men who guided the animals across the prairies were called cowboys.

Cowboys from All Over

If a drive survived the dangers along the way, it was profitable. Cattle might be worth four dollars a head in Texas. In a Kansas cow town, the same animals were worth ten times as much.

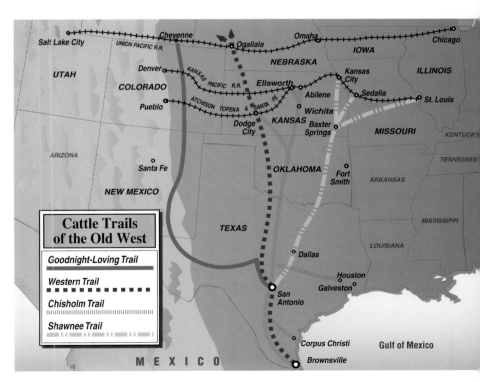

9

As a result, cattle became big business. Roughly thirty thousand cowboys drove some 10 million animals from Texas to Kansas between 1866 and 1890, the "golden era" of the cattle drive.

Drawn by romantic stories of life on the prairie, men came from all over to become cowboys. Some were from midwestern states, others from the urban East. Still more drifted in from other countries such as Ireland and England.

About one-third of the Old West's cowboys were African American, and another third were Hispanic. A few were Native Americans. Despite their ethnic differences, all these men had one thing in common: They were proud to be cowboys.

CHAPTER ONE

Cowboy Dress and Manner

In many ways, cowboys acted and looked alike. All were tough, skinny, and sunburned from working outdoors. They walked stiffly from spending all day in the saddle. They smelled like horses and cattle, and they were dirty most of the time.

Furthermore, they dressed so much alike that everyone knew they were cowboys. They did this on purpose. Cowboys were proud of their jobs, and the clothes a cowboy wore showed that he belonged to a special brotherhood.

At the same time, each cowboy treasured his individuality. Cowboys showed this in many ways. One was to adopt unique nicknames such as "Lippy" or "One-Tooth." Another was to add personal touches, such as a colorful hatband, to the basic cowboy "uniform" of hat, jeans, shirt, vest, and boots.

Hats

Nothing identified a cowboy as quickly as his hat. Hats were such an important part of the cowboy character, it was said, that cowboys took them off only to greet a lady, pray, or sleep.

Cowboy hats had many uses. Their main purpose was to deflect the sun and rain. However, they could also be used to dip water from a stream, carry food to a horse, fan a campfire, or make a signal flag.

Men could look at a cowboy's hat and tell where the wearer came from, because styles varied from place to place. Cowboys in the Southwest, for instance, liked wide brims and high crowns (tops) because they provided shade and coolness. Cowboys on the northern prairies preferred hats with narrow brims and low crowns, because they were less likely to blow away in high winds.

The cowboy's hat has always protected him.

Straw, felt, and leather were the most common materials. Cowboys often decorated fancy dress hats with feathers or embroidery. The most popular hats, made by the John B. Stetson Company, were known for style and long life. Cowboys bragged that their Stetsons looked good even after ten or twenty years of use.

Useful Clothes

All cowboys wore woolen underwear called long johns. In cold weather, long johns were warm. In hot weather, they soaked up sweat that would otherwise have rotted a cowboy's shirt. Long johns had "convenience flaps" so cowboys could relieve themselves without removing their clothes.

Cowboy shirts were plain cotton or wool. They could be any color but red, since many cowboys believed that cattle became angry if they saw red.

Cowboys always wore vests. When a cowboy was in the saddle, items such as tobacco pouches or pocket knives were difficult to find if they were in his pants pockets. Vests had more convenient pockets.

Bandannas, squares of cloth tied loosely around the neck, had many uses, too. They served as dust masks. They protected necks from sunburn and ears from cold winds. They were also used as towels, blindfolds to calm nervous horses, strainers for muddy water, slings for broken arms, or signal flags to far-off comrades.

More Useful Clothes

Most cowboys wore plain wool pants or denim jeans. They did not wear belts or suspenders while working, however; metal buckles cut painfully into their stomachs and suspenders

Cowboys past and present stash important items in vest pockets.

irritated the skin. Instead, cowboys used silk sashes as belts, vaquero style, or simply wore tight-waisted pants.

Over their pants, cowboys wore chaps. These thick leather wrappings protected their legs from scratchy bushes. In cold weather, cowboys sometimes wore "woolies," chaps covered in wool or fur.

Gloves, usually made of leather or horsehide, protected hands from rope burns, wind, sun, thick brush, and insects. Often a cowboy's gloves had long cuffs that protected him almost to the elbow.

For wet weather, cowboys carried canvas raincoats called slickers. Slickers were long enough to cover a man completely and also protect his saddle when he was riding.

Boots and Spurs

The final element in a cowboy's basic outfit was a good pair of leather boots with spurs. Cowboy boots were stylish; they set a man apart from miners, farmers, and any other "tenderfoot" who wore plain, clumsy-looking boots and did not regularly ride a horse.

No cowboy works without thick leather chaps.

At the same time, cowboy boots were practical. Big heels helped a cowboy stay firmly in the saddle, while pointed toes let him slide quickly in and out of his saddle's stirrups. Cowboys needed to be able to get their feet out of stirrups quickly because being dragged behind a runaway horse was a leading cause of death among these riders.

A snug boot was essential for a comfortable ride. Cowboys usually formed a new pair of boots tightly to their feet by wetting them thoroughly and wearing them nonstop for several days. Cowboys wore spurs on their boots. When the cowboys wanted the horses to move they jabbed these sharp metal spikes into the animal's flanks. The unique jingle-jangle sound that

Boots and spurs allow the cowboy more control over his horse.

spurs made as cowboys walked was an important part of their image.

Horses

Clothing was important to a cowboy's self-image and to his work, but his tools and equipment were also important. Most important of all was a good horse. Without a horse, a cowboy was nothing. Trapped on the prairie without one, a traveling cowboy could easily die.

Horses were so important that stealing them was punishable by death. A horse thief captured by cowboys was usually hanged immediately from a nearby tree.

Horses are rounded up to be used on a cattle drive.

Cowboys never rode their own horses on the job, however. Ranch owners felt that cowboys would not run their own horses hard enough, for fear of overtiring or hurting them.

Ranchers therefore provided herds of horses, called **remudas**, from which cowboys chose. Every cowboy changed horses at least once a day, to keep the animals from becoming overworked.

Saddles and Ropes

The Western saddles cowboys used were sturdy. They had heavy knobs on the front, called **horns** or **pommels**, that cowboys tied ropes to when performing chores such as calf roping.

There was a lot of room on Western saddles for carrying belongings. Cowboys could easily tie items such as raincoats, rifles, bedrolls, and **lariats** to their saddles.

Lariats were long, sturdy ropes that had many uses. A cowboy could capture a cow by throwing the looped end of his lariat. By tying the lariat to the horn of his saddle, a cowboy could drag firewood or lead reluctant cattle.

Lariats could also be tied together to form a temporary corral (holding pen) for a herd of horses. On rare occasions, lariats even served as nooses with which to hang horse thieves.

Firearms

Cowboys rarely wore holsters to carry pistols on their hips while working. It was too easy for the gun of a man on horseback to be jarred and accidentally fire.

A cowboy relied mainly on his rifle for hunting and protection from enemies.

Instead, cowboys often kept their six-shooters rolled up in their bedrolls. They used rifles more often, for such purposes as hunting game and protection from enemies.

Cowboys used their tools, clothes, and other possessions every day, all year long, in a regular cycle of work. This annual cycle began with an event called the spring roundup.

CHAPTER TWO

The Roundup

The spring roundup was the busiest part of a cowboy's year. A roundup meant weeks of hard work, but it was also a rare chance for cowboys to see friends from far away.

Roundups were needed because the prairie consisted mainly of open land that belonged to no one. Before barbed wire was invented, cattle roamed freely over this land, searching for grass to eat. They often strayed a hundred or more miles from their home ranch.

In the spring, and sometimes in the fall, cowboys rounded up these strays. They sorted out the animals and returned them to their rightful owners.

Gathering

Every year, word went out that the roundup would begin at a certain ranch. As many as three hundred cowboys from a dozen or more ranches might respond.

Communication and travel were slow, and it might take a week or more for everyone to arrive. During this period before work got under way, however, cowboys could socialize.

A cowboy rounds up a herd of cattle and horses in an open prairie.

They traded news and stories with old friends and got to know new faces. They played card games, sang or danced, and organized contests such as horse racing.

The cowboys were eager to have as much fun as they could. Once the roundup began, there would be no time for anything but hard work, almost round the clock.

Waking Up

Once everyone had arrived, a top cowboy, called the roundup boss, organized the crew into groups and assigned the men to specific sections of land. Each team of fifteen or twenty had a cook and a **chuck wagon**, a portable kitchen where meals were prepared.

A typical day started well before sunup. In the dark, the cowboys climbed out of the bedrolls they had spread on the ground. They pulled on their pants and boots, splashed water on their faces, and ate a quick breakfast around a campfire.

Breakfast was usually pancakes or biscuits and gravy, often with bacon on the side. There was always plenty of strong coffee to help everyone wake up.

The cowboys then chose their first horses of the day, caught them, and saddled up. By daybreak, they were moving out.

Daybreak signals the beginning of a cowboy's long day.

Roundup Mornings

The cowboys rode out from camp in every direction to form a circle many miles across. Then they turned and headed back toward the center. As they rode, they found stray cattle. They drove the animals toward the center by shouting, whistling, and galloping toward them on their horses.

This process was fairly simple if the land was flat, but not in hilly country. Cattle lost or hiding in gullies, ravines, and thickets were hard to find. Also, animals trying to escape were harder to chase. A cowboy might ride fifty to seventy miles in one morning while chasing cattle.

Gradually, however, the cowboys gathered hundreds, sometimes even thousands, of cattle in a concentrated group near camp. As the animals settled down and began to graze, the men ate their midday meal, which they called dinner.

A typical dinner was barbecued beef with biscuits, fried potatoes, and pie for dessert. When a cowboy was done, he scraped his tin plate and put it in a washtub. Then he went back to work.

Identifying the Stock

Several tasks were performed in the afternoon. One was to sort out the cattle that had been collected, making sure that their proper owners were determined. Cattle were identified by brands, special identifying marks burned onto the skin of the cow's side.

Every cattle ranch had a unique brand, which it registered with the county clerk. Hundreds of different brands might be used in a given county.

Cowboys cluster around the chuck wagon for a midday meal.

One man kept a running count of what animals belonged to which ranch. He was called a **tally man**. Ranchers were generally honest with one another about cattle ownership. Sometimes there were disagreements, however. In these cases, the roundup boss acted as a judge.

Cutting Out

Some of the rounded-up animals were calves tagging along after their mothers. These calves, old enough to run but still being nursed by their mothers, belonged to whatever ranch owned the mothers.

The calves needed to be branded for future identification. In order to catch them, they had to be cut out or separated from the herd.

Cutting out calves required a horse that could cooperate closely with its rider. Top cutting horses, ones with good "cow sense," were prized by cowboys.

To cut out a calf, a cowboy first identified its mother. Then he rode quietly into the herd of cattle, being careful not to upset the animals. He directed his horse to nudge the mother cow away from the other cattle. The calf followed close behind.

As the cow moved out of the herd, the cutting horse stayed close behind, nipping at the cow's hindquarters. This kept the cow and calf from returning to the fold.

Branding

Once a calf was away from the herd, the cowboy roped it. He usually did this by bringing his horse close and snagging the calf's hind legs with the loop of his lariat.

The cowboy attached his end of the lariat to his saddle horn and used his horse's strength to help him pull the calf quite close to a waiting fire. There, two other cowboys flipped the animal on its side.

With the calf pinned to the ground, a fourth cowboy used a branding iron, heated red-hot in the fire, to make a mark on its skin, usually the left rear side. The calf moaned and kicked in pain, but the ordeal was over in moments. Teams worked fast: An experienced team could rope and brand dozens of calves an hour.

It was dirty, dangerous work. The area near the fire was hot and dusty. The noise made by the calves was deafening. Furthermore, since the cows were protective of their offspring, the cowboys needed to watch out for attack from the anxious mothers.

A vaquero works quickly to brand a pinned steer.

Ready for Market

The daily routine of work was repeated until a crew finished with one area. Then the crew moved to a new location.

When each crew had found as many cattle as possible, the roundup was complete. Some cattle remained on the ranches where they had been rounded up. Others were returned to their home ranges. Cattle that had grown enough to be ready for market, meanwhile, were kept in a separate herd.

When the work was over, the cowboys celebrated with a big barbecue. Then they got ready for the next step in their yearly cycle: the trail drive.

CHAPTER THREE

The Trail Drive

On a typical trail drive, ten or twelve men drove about twenty-five hundred head of cattle to a market town hundreds of miles away. It was slow going; since herds moved only ten or fifteen miles a day, a drive could take several months.

For most of that time, riding the trail was dull work, a routine of backbreaking labor, boring food, and short sleeping hours. However, the threat of sudden danger was always present.

Different Jobs

The top man on a trail drive was a professional **drover** or trail boss. He was responsible for organizing and leading a drive.

The drover decided such questions as what route to take and how quickly to travel. He rode ahead of the herd, scouting out the day's grazing, watering, and camping sites.

Each cowboy hired by the drover had a specific job. Usually, two point riders rode at the head of the herd, guiding it. Behind them, one on each side of the herd, rode two swing riders and two flank riders. They kept stray cattle from leaving.

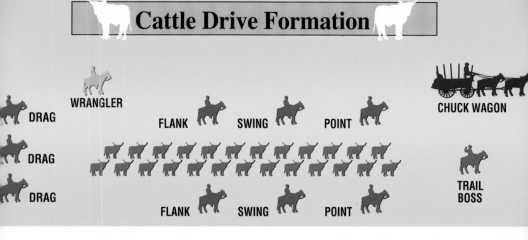

Bringing up the rear were two or three drag riders. Most cowboys felt that riding drag was a terrible job. Even with bandannas protecting their mouths, drag men breathed dust kicked up by thousands of hooves all day. When a drag man shook himself off, huge clouds of dust flew.

The cook, who was often a retired cowboy, drove his chuck wagon ahead of the herd, so that he could prepare meals before the rest arrived. The wrangler, who was responsible for the team's remuda, also helped the cook gather firewood and clean up afterward. Wranglers were often teenagers learning to be cowboys.

Daily Routine

A trail drive's daily routine was quickly established. Everyone was up before daybreak. After a quick breakfast, the point men got the most aggressive cattle moving.

These aggressive cattle naturally took the lead, and the rest of the animals followed. Usually, about five miles could be covered by noon. Then the cowboys broke for dinner, at a spot chosen by the drover. Dinner rarely lasted more than an hour—just long enough for the men to eat and for the horses and cattle to graze a little.

The group would then push on until about 5 P.M. The signal to stop for the night was given by the trail boss, who rode down the line waving his hat. It was always a welcome sight.

Roundup Evenings

The men slowed the cattle down, let them drink water out of a stream, then herded them into a circle. The animals then lay down and settled for the night. Meanwhile, the cook had started his fire and was preparing the evening meal.

After eating, the crew gathered around a campfire. They told stories, smoked, or talked about people they knew and places they had seen. If someone had a harmonica or a fiddle, there would be music and singing.

Everyone went to sleep early, however. All were tired, and some knew they would be awakened for guard duty later. The cowboys took turns at this. Usually there were two guards at a time, with several shifts each night.

Guards rode slowly around the quiet cattle in opposite directions. As they rode, they sang, because they knew that the human voice kept cows calm. Singing was so important to the job that many trail bosses refused to hire cowboys who did not have good singing voices.

A cowboy guards the cattle at night by circling slowly around the herd.

Trail Food

The food that a drive's cook provided every day was hearty but boring. He was limited to ingredients that could be stored in his chuck wagon, such as beans, dried apples, bacon, and salt pork.

Once in a while, he could vary the basic diet. Sometimes he found a patch of herbs to enliven a stew, or a

A huge dinner of stew and biscuits is cooked on an open fire in iron skillets.

cowboy shot a jackrabbit or other game. With luck, a trail boss might trade a newborn calf to a farmer for eggs or vegetables. The cowboys would have left such a calf behind, anyway, since it could not have kept up with the herd.

Although they were guiding thousands of cattle, cowboys never ate beef on the trail. The meat spoiled quickly, and even one animal produced too much beef for a twenty-man crew. Besides, the animals would be far too valuable at the end of the trail.

No matter what the men ate, there was always plenty of coffee. It helped them stay alert during the long workdays and the nights of too little sleep. Cowboys preferred "six-shooter coffee"—a brew so strong that they claimed it could float a six-shooter.

Danger

Even though most days on the trail were routine, cowboys were always alert to danger. The worst threat was from cattle stampedes.

A herd could be frightened by something big, such as lightning, or by something small, such as a rattlesnake, bobcat, or owl darting around in darkness. If frightened, the cattle could suddenly start running in a group.

Stampeding cattle trampled everything in their way, including slower animals and careless cowboys. To stop them, cowboys tried to control the lead cattle by firing their guns in the air. They hoped to turn the stampede in a circle until the animals stopped from exhaustion.

Another danger was a swift river that could drown a man and his horse while they crossed it. Quicksand trapped many men, wagons, and animals. Other perils included poisonous snakes and scorpions, lightning storms, and broken ground that crippled horses when it caused them to stumble, twisting or breaking a leg.

Some threats were human. Rustlers might deliberately stampede a herd, so that they could steal strays in the aftermath. Some Indian tribes attacked cowboys because they were angry about invasions of their land. Also, farmers often attacked trail drives because they feared diseases that cattle could carry.

End of the Trail

The cowboys were delighted when they finally reached the end of the trail—a Kansas cow town. The trail boss could then sell the herd there and pay his crew anywhere from fifty to one hundred dollars each.

This was what the cowboys had been waiting for. Even a town with no running water, no indoor plumbing, and no sidewalks seemed heavenly after months on the trail.

The barbershop was the first stop for most cowboys after being paid. Barbers usually had tubs in a back room, so a cowboy could soak the months of grime and sweat off before getting a trim and a shave. Also important was a stop at a general store, where the men could buy new clothes and throw away their old ones.

After that, they were ready for fun. Music halls, gambling parlors, and bars were three places where a cowboy could spend his money. Posing for a souvenir photograph was also popular. And some women were happy to entertain cowboys who had not seen a female in months.

Cowboys gamble at a card table.

Typically, cowboys spent most of their earnings quickly. If they were lucky, there was enough left over to buy a horse each. Then they could head south again and look for work over the coming winter.

CHAPTER FOUR

Back at
the Ranch

After the trail drive, some cowboys returned to the same ranch year after year. Others preferred to find new ranches.

Generally, ranches did not need many workers over the winter. They could afford to keep only skeleton crews and hired only experienced cowboys.

Younger cowboys found jobs such as washing dishes or tending bar in town. Others "rode the grub line," riding from ranch to ranch and doing odd jobs in exchange for a meal and a place to sleep.

For cowboys who were hired by a rancher over the winter, life was mainly performing routine chores. However, it was work as a cowboy—which, for many, was still the best life.

Bunkhouse Life

Most cowboys on smaller ranches typically did not have houses of their own. They lived in the main ranch house with the ranch owner and his family.

On larger ranches, however, cowboys had separate buildings called bunkhouses. A bunkhouse could be just a shack with a dirt floor and bug-infested mat-

Bronco busting is a routine chore for a cowboy.

tresses. It could also be a solid building with a fireplace and its own kitchen and dining facilities.

The sleeping quarters were usually one large room. Each cowboy spread his bedroll on a bunk, stored his possessions in a trunk underneath, and hung his clothes on nails in the wall.

Whether in the rancher's house or the bunkhouse, a cowboy could count on hearty meals. Unlike the trail drives, when slaughtering cattle would have wasted meat, ranches routinely killed cattle for their crews.

Cowboys generally liked beef and ate it several times a day, if they could. Other bunkhouse staples included

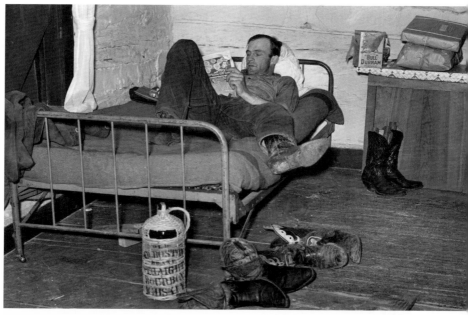

After a hard day's work, a cowboy stretches out on his bunk.

bacon, biscuits, beans, preserved fruits and vegetables from the rancher's garden—and, of course, coffee.

Chores

As on the trail, a cowboy's day began before sunrise. The first man up would start the stove to take the edge off the morning chill.

By the time everyone had shaved and dressed, the cook had breakfast ready. A typical morning meal might be scrambled eggs, fried tomatoes, biscuits, ham, sausage, corn bread, and coffee.

Everyone ate quickly and started work by sunup. The cowboys caught and saddled their first horses, and the rancher or his foreman assigned jobs. These typically included splitting and hauling firewood, repairing corrals and fences, treating sick or injured animals, fixing saddles and bridles, and maintaining wagons and other equipment.

Some cowboys also spent time **bronco busting,** "breaking" (taming) horses so that they could be trained and ridden. Bronco busting was a special skill, and only a few cowboys excelled at it.

A cowboy gets a physical workout "breaking" a bronco.

Riding Out

Another routine job was to ride a section of the ranch and watch for stray cattle. This cut down on the number of cattle that needed to be found in spring.

If a cowboy found a sick or injured animal, he roped it and treated it as best he could with medicines he always carried. Sometimes he had to bring the injured animal back to the ranch for more treatment.

Sick or injured cattle in the herd must be cared for.

Sometimes, cowboys had to rescue animals that became stuck in wet, boggy land, by tying ropes around the animals' necks and pulling them free. They also had to check the watering holes that cattle used, clearing out any debris with a shovel or chopping through ice so the animals could drink.

It was especially important to ride the range after storms. Driving snow and wind often forced cows to drift for miles. Cowboys had to find them and bring them home, using their horses to make paths through the snow that the cows could follow.

Riding the Line

Very large ranches were too big to be controlled from a single base. In this case, ranchers established **line camps**. These were bases from which cowboys could patrol distant areas.

Line camps were usually primitive. Sometimes they were simple huts made of packed dirt or logs, with buffalo hides on the walls for insulation.

A cowboy assigned to a line camp rode the edges of his territory daily and kept cattle from drifting away. He also watched out for dangers both human (such as rustlers) and natural (such as wolves).

Riding the line was a lonely job. Often a cowboy lived for weeks or even months by himself or with only one other cowboy. His only pastimes might be a supply of tobacco, a deck of cards, and a stack of "dime novels," cheap and popular adventure stories. This solitary life suited some cowboys well, but others complained they missed "jawing" (talking) with their friends.

Cowboys riding line camp find cattle that stray from the herd.

Off Hours

Most ranches were far from any town. An injured cowboy could not expect to see a doctor.

Instead, he used home remedies. Brown paper soaked in vinegar was often wrapped around a sprained ankle. Cuts and other wounds were treated with axle grease or a paste made of spit and chewing tobacco.

Because they were so far from town, cowboys also relied on themselves for entertainment. In the evenings, sitting near the wood stove, they often played card games such as poker. Those who could read did so, often out loud, since many cowboys had little education and did not know how to read.

Cowboys had other amusements for their days off. If the weather was fine, they could fish or hunt. Another favorite pastime was playing practical jokes; one classic was taking off a horse's saddle and putting it on backward when the rider was not watching.

Cowboys also loved competitions, such as racing their horses, shooting at targets, and testing other skills. One favorite contest involved leaning from a horse at full gallop and picking up coins from the ground.

No More to Ramble

Drinking was not a normal pastime on a ranch, since many ranchers did not permit alcohol on the job. However, on those rare occasions when a cowboy could go to town—which might be only twice a year—most cowboys liked to drink.

Cowboys might also attend a dance at a neighboring ranch a few times a year. Men looked forward to these special times for weeks in advance, carefully cleaning themselves up and wearing their fanciest clothes.

Dances gave lonely cowboys a rare chance to meet women—if they were lucky, perhaps they met their future wives. The cowboys would then have companions when they were ready to settle down.

Settling down, perhaps with ranches of their own, was what most cowboys did as they got older. Being a cowboy was a job for the young and strong. Some became cooks or otherwise stayed close to the cowboy life all their lives. Others chose less strenuous ways of living out their remaining years. Almost all of them, however, looked back on their cowboy days with pleasure.

Glossary

bronco busting: "Breaking" (taming) horses so that they could be trained and ridden.

chuck wagon: A wagon adapted for use as a portable cooking stove and place to store food.

cutting out: Separating a calf and its mother from the herd so that it could be branded.

drover: A professional who was responsible for organizing, planning, and leading a trail drive.

horn (pommel): The post on the front of a Western saddle. Cowboys tied their lariats to them when dragging firewood or pulling cattle.

lariat: A long rope, often looped so that cowboys could "lasso" (make a slipknot and capture) cattle.

line camp: An isolated camp used as a base when patrolling distant parts of a large ranch.

remuda: The herd of horses from which cowboys chose their mounts. From the Spanish word for "replacement," since cowboys used several horses a day to keep from overtiring any one animal.

tally man: A cowboy who kept track during a roundup of what cattle belonged to which ranch.

vaqueros: Early Mexican cowboys, who lent the North American cowboys many of their customs and methods.

For Further Exploration

Russell Freedman, *Children of the Old West.* New York: Clarion Books, 1983. A clearly written book with terrific period photographs.

—————, *Cowboys of the Old West.* New York: Clarion Books, 1985. A companion to Freedman's book on children of the Old West.

William Manns and Elizabeth Clair Flood, *Cowboys and the Trappings of the Old West.* Santa Fe, NM: Zon International, 1997. A large-format book, heavily illustrated, focusing on the equipment and clothing of old-time cowboys.

David H. Murdoch, *Cowboy.* New York: Knopf/ Dorling Kindersley, 1993. This is an excellent source for details about cowboys from different parts of the world.

Peter Newark, *Cowboys.* New York: Exeter Books, 1983. A well-illustrated and detailed look at this fascinating subject..

Martin W. Sandler, *Cowboys.* New York: HarperCollins, 1994. This book, sponsored by the Library of Congress, is notable mainly for its wonderful illustrations detailing a cowboy's life.

Index

Picture Credits

About the Author

Adam Woog is the author of more than thirty books for adults, teens, and children. His books for Lucent Books include volumes on Harry Houdini, Elvis Presley, Steven Spielberg, Amelia Earhart, FDR and the New Deal, and the Beatles. He lives with his wife and daughter in his hometown of Seattle, Washington.